The Wisdom of Wildflowers and the Magic of Moonlight

Dawn Weast

The Wisdom of Wildflowers and the Magic of Moonlight © 2023 Dawn Weast

All rights reserved.

No part of this publication may be reproduced, stored in a retrieval system, or transmitted, in any form or by any means, electronic, mechanical, photocopying, recording, or otherwise, without the prior written permission of the presenters.

Dawn Weast asserts the moral right to be identified as the author of this work.

Presentation by *BookLeaf Publishing*

Web: www.bookleafpub.com

E-mail: info@bookleafpub.com

ISBN: 9789358368246

First edition 2023

This book is dedicated to Allen, my husband, who finds all the good places to explore. Also, to my boys, Alex, Brady, Colton, Eiden, and Finn who inspire me every day with their shenanigans. Thank you, and I love you all!

The Wisdom of Wildflowers

There's wisdom in wildflowers
It can be seen in how they grow
Yearning toward the sun in spring

It is in the feeding of the bees
The year's first sweet nectar
The balance with each living thing

There's wisdom in wildflowers
Leaves, then buds, swiftly grow
Riotous color brightens the gloom

The snow barely recedes
Then beauty after winter's gray
Silent persistence in every bloom

There's wisdom in wildflowers
Despite the flash of brilliance
It's subtle, quiet, and still

Reminding us that the wheel turns
And even though each bud dies
The hope of Spring never will

Wild Winter Rose

In the bitter cold
The ice wind bites
Where they say no flower grows
One stands alone
With strength unknown
The wild winter rose

Head held high
And leaves of green
Snowflakes on its thorns
Softest petals
Rival hardest metals
When fighting out the storms

The surest sign
Of strength within
Is never where it shows
Standing alone
Your strength unknown
Wild Winter Rose

After the Rain Has Gone Away

The days are cold and dreary
The clouds obscure the skies
My heart grows ever weary
As rain falls from my eyes

I long for summer sunshine
To chase away the gray
I know that love will be mine
After the rain has gone away

We'll sing under the starlight
And dance beneath the moon
We'll play away the warm night
I hope those days come soon

I sing of sunny weather
And watch the stormy day
And dream of days together
After the rain has gone away

Yes, I sing of sunny weather
And dream about the day
I know we'll laugh together
After the rain has gone away

July

The warm wind blows
The verdant trees sway
And gray river ripples
Are chasing the day

Blackberry breeze
Perfumes humid air
Lush memories
Bursting to share

Tufts like snowflakes
Cottonwood flower
Drift on the airflow
A swirling shower

Barefoot and horseback
A picnic of plums
Shared treasures
Dripping down thumbs

Warm July wind
Gone in a flash
Scents of a moment
Summer a dash

Fantasy

Pan play your pipes
And Bacchus bring the wine
We'll dance among the trees
And have a very fine time

Two children ran into the forest
To play a silly game
They saw a wood nymph passing by
And stopped to ask her name

My name is Woodling Heather
I'm off to a jamboree
Come to a fairy party
And dance the night with me

We'll eat up the starlight
We'll drink the morning dew
If tomorrow ever comes
We'll start again brand new

Unicorn play your horn
And moon shine down bright
We'll dance among the trees
And sing all through the night

Imagination is a Place

Imagination is a place
Where the forgotten children go
To dwell in a realm of make-believe
With the creatures that they know

Where no secret fears sneak
When the children do not see
Where all their joys emerge
Where they can just be

Imagination is a place
Where the forgotten children go
To let their souls fly free
Where love and dreams flow

Where all horrors are beaten
When they sing a merry song
Where dreams are within reach
Where their lives are happy and long

Imagination is a place
Where the forgotten children go
To be all they could wish
Where no winds of sadness blow

Where the forgotten ones remember
Where they are the only ones that know
The world that has forgotten them
Is the one that made imagination grow

Live The Life

Live the life of the prophet's tales
Pursue the path of destiny
Bow to the gods of all men
Go after the dream that's free

Gallop the trodden trail
Trundle the narrow lane
Walk in the way of knowledge
Be content and be sane

Follow your father's footsteps
Tag after mom's apron strings
Do what brother and sister do
Wait and see what tomorrow brings

Or…

Laugh at the prophets and their tales
And fate and destiny
Show the gods what is faith
Be blissful and be free

Stroll down the trail less traveled
Race down a wider lane
Skip along the way of wisdom
Be happy and insane

Measure your father's footsteps
Cut those apron strings
Don't worry about brother and sister
And make what tomorrow brings

Friends are Memories

Friends are memories that do not fade
They remain vivid and fresh to the eye
Though years may pass, and lives may change
Some things shared will never die

So, look at friends through rose-colored glasses
See gap-toothed grins and skinned-up knees
Remember the days of running through
sprinklers
Freeze tag, and hanging from apricot trees

Find a day that you cherish and the friend behind
it
The puddles you splashed and the bikes you
rode
Remember just who it is that you think of
As you travel down life's lonely road

The words you made up that mean nothing at all
And the ones that mean more than can be said
The games that were played, they seem silly
now
The fun we had then, would turn our faces red

In the eyes of our friends, we see more than just
love
We see acceptance, laughter, and sheer disbelief
For only a friend understands those things
That bring our hearts such utter relief

Our friends are memories that do not fade
They remain ever agreeable to the eye
Though years may pass, and lives may change
Some things shared never do pass us by

Questions

What good's a heart
Without a romance
How can music move me
If I refuse to dance
Where do I hide
A dream that I adore
When do you find out
If there is anything more

If I close my eyes
Will I see eternity
If I change my name
Will I still be me
If I run so fast
That the world fades away
Will I learn the answers
To yesterday

Can you tell me why
Love is full of pain
Can you show me how
The clouds bring the rain
Can you find me a melody
That will make me cry
Can you build me a passion
To make me try

How can I see tomorrow
When today is gone
Will I see the darkness
After the dawn
Can I know the reasons
But not know the rhyme
Who can tell the passage
Of their own time

What is the point
Of hope or destiny
When do we find out
What it means to be free
Where is the purpose
In each shining star
Why do we always seek
To find who we are

Storms

Some people live their lives
With cloud shadows
Hiding their innermost thoughts
And feelings behind a mask
Of fluffy white composure
Yet, sometimes,
The heat is too much
And a spectacular storm results
Lightening and thunder reign
Wind whips and rain falls
The tension is released
In all its fury…

… I like storms.

Sweetest Love

If I had to choose, just one love;
Be I mother, friend, or wife.
The choice between man, woman, or child;
Lover, sister, or life.
How could I choose, without a taste
Of how each love can be?
And should I choose, if each of them
Could fall in love with me?
Once tasted sweets, shall I crave,
A love that's sweeter still?
Shall I despair, to ever choose,
The one my tastes will fill?
I think no one choice, could be enough,
To keep me satisfied.
For, not any love, no one the same;
Can be passed on, once it's tried!

The Duel

Steam rises, blood boils
A heart is on the line
Ten paces, shots fired
Her scream is frozen in time

Two brothers, one woman
There was bound to be a duel
One heart, two loves
What was to be the rule

Despairing, not knowing
Just how to stop the fight
She's running, they're turning
Two shots split the night

Smoke clears, hearts stop
Two brothers eye to eye
Guns drop, both run
For she is going to die

Tears run, both ask
Why she stepped in the way
Eyes closed, lips moved
Only one thing she could say

She loved, she wronged
She was too weak to choose
Time heals, blood bonds
She had the least to lose

She sighs, she knows
As she slowly slips away
Two brothers, one woman
There is always hell to pay

The Ballad of the Unicorn

Away upon a sun-kissed hill
There ran so wild and free
A creature made of light and love
Coursing untamed as the sea

Starlight shown from his eyes
The moonbeams were his mane
Magic sparked his silver horn
No mortals knew his name

Until a dawn painted the sky
More perfect than any other
A young maid wept upon the loam
For her fallen brother

So moved by this sad sweet sound
He could not run away
The creature watched over her
As dawn turned into day

At last the maid was still
Her tears at last all shed
When she felt whisper soft kisses
Upon her grief-bowed head

Looking up she saw the creature
So bright it out-shone the sun
She thought it was an angel
And her days on earth were done

But the creature was so still
As it studied the sad child
Knowing not what manner of Fairy
Sat here in the wild

The girl reached up a hand
Toward his brow, his spiral horn
Then she whispered a name
Daring to call him 'Unicorn'

He reared back and began to run
She smiled through tears all dry
The day the unicorn stopped
To watch a maiden cry

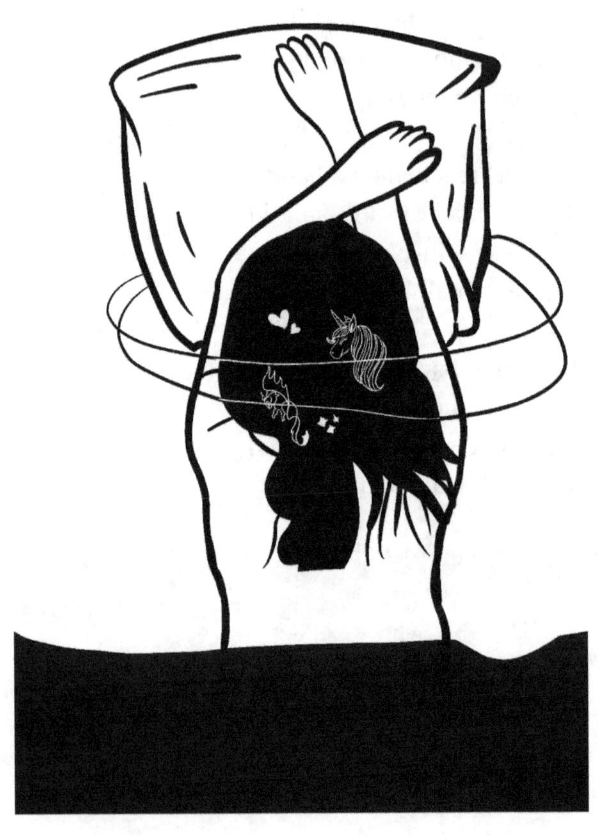

Wishing Star

Once upon a time quite far
I wished upon a shining star

And even though no dreams came true
I'm still a dreamer through and through

And every place I've gone since then
I've wished upon that star again

I will wish and hope and dream
So long as I have breath to scream

At stars that twinkle in the night
Or blown wishes taking flight

Because sometimes hope is all I've got
And sometimes wishes can't be bought

So I'll dream a little dream and then
I'll wish upon that star again

I Dare Not Dream

I dare not dream
Beyond a cloud
I dare not hope
Right out loud

I should not wish
For heart's desire
I could not plead
With raging fire

I have not tried
To rope the wind
I have not cried
Until the end

I could not rage
or fall apart
I would not crush
A fragile heart

I will never fall
With a broken wing
I'll never fail
If I never sing

I dare not dream
Beyond a cloud
I dare not hope
Right out loud

Have You Ever

Have you ever wanted happily ever after
Almost knowing it is achievable
That somewhere time will stand still
And you will have the unbelievable

Have you ever looked for a glass slipper
When you found it did it fit like a glove
Just the perfect thing at the perfect time
A feeling that's something a lot like love

Have you ever chased down a rainbow
Those hues so solid yet not even there
Driven so far that you almost touched
The magic of brilliant diamond air

Have you ever searched for unicorns
In the soft shadows of a forest glade
A vision of absolute grace so amazing
It pierces your soul like a blade

Have you ever sought a fairy tale
That you could call your very own
It may be the hunt that matters most
As the tapestry of dreams is sewn

IF

If hope were a hilltop
I'd wish for high mountains
If dreams were droplets
I'd wish for whole fountains
If time was sand
I'd wish for great dunes
If faith were a note
I'd wish for sweet tunes
If kisses were raindrops
I'd wish for warm showers
If friends were a second
I'd wish for long hours
If devotion were salt
I'd wish for the sea
If love were a person
I'd wish you with me

Lullaby

The stars are shining brightly
The moon is glowing too
The wind is singing softly
A sweet lullaby for you
While you slumber darling
You will dream of a faery land
And build a shining castle
From golden grains of sand
Dance among the elves
And sing a mermaid's song
Ride a silver unicorn
All the nighttime long
Fly on a magic carpet
Made of rainbow light
Softly you will slumber
As your dreams take flight
So rest your little head
And close those big bright eyes
Listen to the night song
Sing you lullabies
And I'll be ever near you
Til the morning light
With windsong melodies
Whispering all the night

The Wolf and The Rose

The wolf howls at the silver moon
Yet, to him it will not descend
He can't see it's a reflection
A sterile far-flung friend

And still, he searches on and on
Over heather, heath, and loam
Through the deep green forests
In the darkness he will roam

He can't find what he seeks
In every cold black night
He doesn't know what he's after
So blinded by moonlight

For the folly of a lonely wolf
Is sight and smell dismissed
For a bright glamour in the sky
Ephemeral as the morning mist

He doesn't know he need not seek
What he wants is under his nose
Sometimes a wolf is too blind to see
The moon shines down on a rose

Wanderlust

A pulling, tugging, wrenching
Feeling not unknown
Something is calling me
Far away from home

Across the vast oceans
To adventures unseen
Leading me places
That I've never been

Pyramids and towers
Forests, fields, and sands
Any place can be
Where my heart lands

Whispering so softly
Of mysteries to explore
Somewhere in that world
Beyond my front door

A calling so insistent
For me to come find
All the wondrous places
I can see inside my mind

The Magic of Moonlight

Gazing out my window
The stars are all alight
The trees are singing softly
Of the magic of moonlight

In times that used to be
For my own delight
I'd hearken to those trees
And the magic of moonlight

I remember running wild
Down paths that still invite
Chasing, ever racing
The magic of moonlight

Floating through the forests
My soul taking flight
Finding all my joy
In the magic of moonlight

Now I sit waiting
For my sweet little sprite
To grow their own wings
In the magic of moonlight